MW01128310

This Journal Belongs To:

110 Page, Wide Ruled 6" x 9"
Blank Lined Journal

Made in the USA
Las Vegas, NV
29 February 2024

86429411R00066